Kobus Genis

MW01599771

MEET
GOD

Through the LETTERS

MODULE 1

In memory of my parents, Koos and Malie Genis, who instilled the love for the Bible in me.

CONTENTS

INTRODUCTION

Video material of all lessons is available at
https://biblegps.teachable.com

Our journey through life often leads us on unknown paths. We know that life can have rather sharp edges and that pain and sorrow are part of our existence. It is therefore not always easy to find our way in life. We can feel a little bit lost and lonely.

The good news is that God has given us a GPS to find our way through life – God's Word, our God Positioning System. According to Psalm 119:105, God's Word is a lamp to our feet and a light for our path.

Erwin McManus started his book *"An Unstoppable Force"* with a striking quote:

"The vast ocean of the unknown can only be navigated through the compass of an ancient text."

The Bible, as ancient text, has passed the test of time. No other book has influenced humanity more than the Bible.

The Bible outstrips any other as the world's all-time bestseller. It remains so popular today, thousands of years after it was first written, that it is excluded from bestseller lists the world over so that it doesn't skew the charts. And yet, an increasing number of people are not reading the Bible.

The Bible helps us to stay on course. In reality, many people still believe in the gospel but do not know how to apply the message of the Bible on their life journey. So many people have told me that they started reading the Bible with great enthusiasm but that their enthusiasm did not last long because they found it difficult to understand. Some told me that they felt completely lost in the Bible. This is actually the last place you want to be lost—it is, after all, God's Word!

Why is it not always easy to understand the Bible? This is because the time, culture and circumstances of the READER (people of the 21st century) and the SENDER (writers of the Bible) are quite different.

This course teaches you the method which will help you to bridge these differences. This method is known as the **Bible GPS** (**G**od **P**ositioning **S**ystem).

The *BIBLE GPS* will be your guide to help you to navigate through the Bible and to **meet God** on your journey. The Bible was never meant to merely inform us; the Bible was meant to _____ us.

The Global Positioning System (GPS) is probably one of the best inventions of our time. It helps you to find your way and not get lost!

How does the Bible GPS-Method work?

Bible GPS equips you with 3 steps to help you understand the Bible. These steps are the processes of **UNDERSTANDING**, **APPLICATION** and **COMMUNICATION**. You are going to master these skills. It's not difficult!

UNDERSTANDING:

The purpose of this is to determine how the original recipients (first readers) understood a passage.

The process of UNDERSTANDING consists of five steps and the first letters of these steps spell the word _____.

The five steps are:

Situation

Type of literature

Analysis of the passage

Relationship to the rest of the Bible

Test of your findings

APPLICATION:

In this process, we determine whether that message to the original receiver still APPLIES to us or not.

COMMUNICATION:

If it does apply to us, we determine how to **COMMUNICATE** it in our time.
I would like to give you a **preview** of what you can expect in the course. I want to do it by taking you on a test drive. In the test drive, I will demonstrate the 3 steps by analyzing Ephesians 2: 1-10.

In the process of analysis, we group words and thoughts that go together. It helps us to see how the author has arranged his thoughts. If someone talks about a "hole in one", "club", "greens" and "handicap", then we know that the conversation is about golf.

Are your ready? Fasten your seatbelts!

Let's read the first three verses of Ephesians 2. Note that all the underlined words that Paul uses are related.

¹As for you, you <u>were dead</u> in your <u>transgressions</u>
and <u>sins</u>,
²in which you used to live
when you <u>followed the ways of this world</u>
and of <u>the ruler of the kingdom of the air</u>,
<u>the spirit</u> who is <u>now at work</u>
in those who are <u>disobedient.</u>
³All of us also lived among them at one time,
<u>gratifying the cravings</u> of our <u>sinful nature</u>
<u>and following its desires</u> and <u>thoughts.</u>
Like the rest, we were by nature <u>objects of wrath.</u>

All the underlined words are interrelated and refer to a _____!

From verse 4, there is a change in Paul's thinking. The change was introduced by the word "but". In any conversation, you need to listen carefully when someone uses the word "but" because what follows is what the person really wants to communicate.

In verses 4-9, we note that Paul uses words that belong together.

> ⁴But because of his <u>great love</u> for us,
> God, who is <u>rich in mercy</u>,
> ⁵<u>made us alive</u> <u>with Christ</u>
> even when we were dead in transgressions—
> it is <u>by grace you have been saved</u>.
> ⁶And <u>God raised us up with Christ</u>
> <u>and seated us with him</u>
> in <u>the heavenly realms in Christ Jesus</u>,
> ⁷in order that in the coming ages
> he <u>might show</u> <u>the incomparable riches</u> of <u>his grace</u>,
> expressed in his <u>kindness</u> to us <u>in Christ Jesus.</u>
> ⁸For it is <u>by grace you have been saved</u>,
> <u>through faith</u>—and this <u>not from yourselves</u>,
> it is the <u>gift of God</u>—
> ⁹<u>not by works</u>,
> so that no one can boast.

_____

_____

Verses 4 to 9 flooded us with positive thoughts. It describes a _____ **GOD**, who helps us out of the BIG MESS.

Verse 10 again draws attention to our responsibility.

> ¹⁰For <u>we</u> are <u>God's workmanship</u>,
> <u>created in Christ Jesus</u> <u>to do good works</u>,
> <u>which God prepared in advance</u> <u>for us</u> <u>to do</u>.

_____

_____

(New International Version)

It refers to a golden _____ we have to make a difference in the world.

The process of analysis helps us discover how the author has arranged his thoughts.

VERSES 1-3	VERSES 4-9	VERSE 10
What a Mess	What a GOD	What an Opportunity
G_____	G_____	G_____
S_____	S_____	S_____

Interestingly, all Paul's letters follow this classification. Paul starts with the bad news to serve as a backdrop for the good news. The good news inspires us to do good works, not to be saved, but because we are grateful for our salvation by grace. I hope you enjoyed the test drive!

Lesson 1 deals with how the Bible came into existence. You will once again realize that no other book equals the Bible.

Lesson 2 deals with the Overview of the Bible. It is important to form a complete picture of the Bible. If you, for example, are in New York, you know that you are about 4490 km from Los Angeles, CA and about 347 km from Boston, MA.

Lesson 3 covers the different types of literature of the Bible. The Bible writers have different ways to communicate the message (e.g. stories, poems and parables). It is important to identify the type of literature being read because each is being read in a different way. You do for example not read a poem like a story.

In **Lesson 4** we are going to master the GPS-Method. It comprises of the Processes of Understanding, Application and Communication.

In **Lessons 5** we will get a better understanding of Epistles / Letters.

In **Lessons 6-7** we will apply the GPS-Method on two passages from the Epistles.

Objective of Module 1

To be able to master the three processes of the Bible GPS.

How do we accomplish this?

• You will learn how the original reader / receiver understood the message.

• You will learn whether the message to the original recipient is applicable to us in the 21st century or not.

• You will learn how to communicate the message in the 21st century.

• You are going to practice the GPS skills on two passages.

Enjoy the journey!

LESSON 1
HOW DID THE BIBLE COME INTO BEING?

Purpose
To be amazed about the uniqueness of the Bible

Why should we have some understanding of how the Bible came to us?
- to realize that the Bible, like creation, is an _____.

Why do we say that?
- although it was written on three continents (_____, _____ and _____),
- in three different languages (_____, _____ and _____),
- over a period of about _____ years,
- by more than _____ authors (from all walks of life),
- the Bible as a whole forms a _____.

This unit makes the Bible _____ among all books.

The Bible did not just simply drop from the sky, but it came into being through a fascinating, but complicated _____.

To best understand the process we need to be aware of:

- The _____

- The _____

- The _____

1. The Two Traditions

The Bible evolved over a time span of approximately 1500 years. The time span can be divided into an _____ **tradition** and a _____**tradition**.

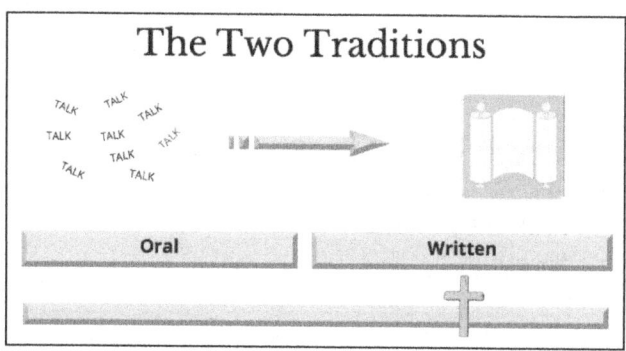

The oral tradition lasted for _____ as families passed along the stories of their ancestors to each new generation before they were written down in a final form. The oral tradition is likely dated to the time of Abraham, around 1800 BC.

The oral tradition has **steadily** _____ into written tradition as societies in the Near East began to develop the art of writing. Probably the **first** written parts of Scripture were short pieces of _____, dating to the time of the exodus around 1300 BC.

2. The Languages

Most of the original manuscripts of the Old Testament were written in
_____, although a few chapters of Ezra and Daniel were recorded in
_____ (dialect of Hebrew), the language spoken by Jesus.

The New Testament was written in the first century AD in _____
because it was the most spoken language around the Mediterranean at the
time.

| Did you know that the first book ever printed was the Bible?

Who do you think decided which books would be part of the Bible?

_____

3. The Councils

Who decided which books would be part of the Bible?

Three **church** _____ (synods) played a very important role to determine which books needed to be in the Bible.

They were:

a) _____ (± 90 AD)

b) _____ (± 397 AD)

c) _____ (± 1546 AD)

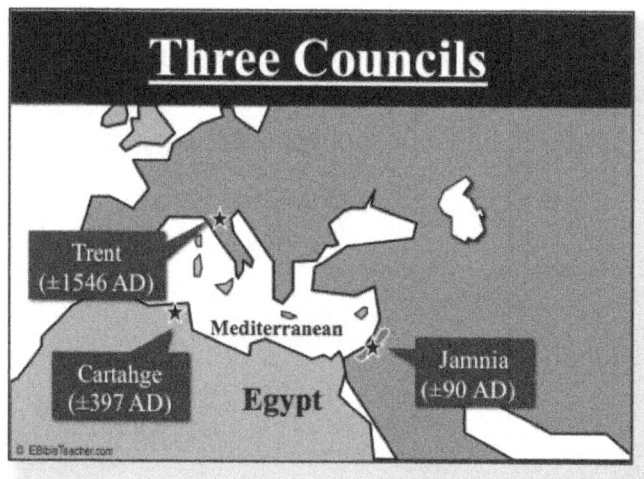

a) The Council of Jamnia (±90 AD)

At Jamnia, in Palestine, the _____ formally recognized the sacred Jewish writings of the Old Testament as the official version of the Hebrew Bible.

The Jewish Bible contains the same books as the Old Testament of the Protestant Bible.

b) The Council of Carthage (±397 AD)

The Council of Carthage (located on the north Coast of Africa in the city of Tunis, Tunisia) was the official gathering of _____ bishops (leaders) gave their formal approval to the _____ books which made up the New Testament.

c) The Council of Trent (±1546 AD)

500 years ago, a German monk named Martin Luther started a protest against the Roman Catholic Church that exploded into worldwide movement. At that time, Europe lived in the shadow of the Roman Catholic Church. It was more like an empire than a church.

The Council of Trent (in northern Italy) was a gathering of _____ to reply to the growing Protestants Reformation.

At this Council the Roman Catholics added _____ extra books to the Old Testament. The emerging Protestants did not want to include these books into the Bible since they did not regard them as inspired.

However, Protestants, Roman Catholics, and Greek Orthodox Christians _____ on the same 27 books for the composition of the New Testament.

General Remarks

- **Where does the name "Bible" come from?**

The word Bible comes from the Greek biblia, meaning "_____".

- **What do you tell someone who says the Bible cannot be trusted because you only have copies?**

Although we don't have the original manuscripts of the Bible, we do have _____ that still exist today e.g. the Leningrad Codex, or *Leningradensis,* the oldest complete Hebrew Bible still preserved, the Dead Sea Scrolls and
the **Codex Vaticanus** which is an almost complete New Testament and has been at the Vatican Library since 1475.

- **What do you tell someone that says that the Bible cannot be trusted because you only have copies?**

I think you could answer that with a counter question:

Of what do you make copies? **You make copies of the things that are _____ to you**. The process of making copies of the original manuscripts were very expensive and were done with great precision.

Did you know that with the possible exception of a few pages of Sir Thomas More, a play that Shakespeare may have helped write, no manuscripts of Shakespeare's survive? Yet, I have heard of no person who doubted the work of Shakespeare.

- **Why is the Bible divided into two parts: The Old Testament and The New Testament?**

Since there is a _____ - year gap between the last book of the Old Testament and the first book of the New Testament, the Bible is divided up into those two parts.

- **Why are the two parts called a 'Testament'?**

The word testament is a derivation of the Latin word testamentum, which was used to translate the Hebrew for _____. The word has come to be used in describing the two main divisions of the Bible. It should be understood, then, that the Bible is generally to be looked at as a covenant. A covenant is an agreement between two parties, and in the Bible it is an agreement between God and humanity.

- **Why aren't books being added to the Bible in modern day?**

The widely held belief is that the Bible as the inspired word of God is a _____ work. If the Scripture we already have is perfect, sure, right, pure, clean, and true, why would we need more? Why would we seek more? The Scripture already revealed by God can make us complete for everything God has called us to be and do in life.

We see that the Bible did not merely drop from the sky, but came into being by a fascinating, yet _____ **process**.

No other book has such a history. No other book has influenced humanity more than the Bible. For believers, it is indeed God's Word that gives life!

How did the Bible come into being?

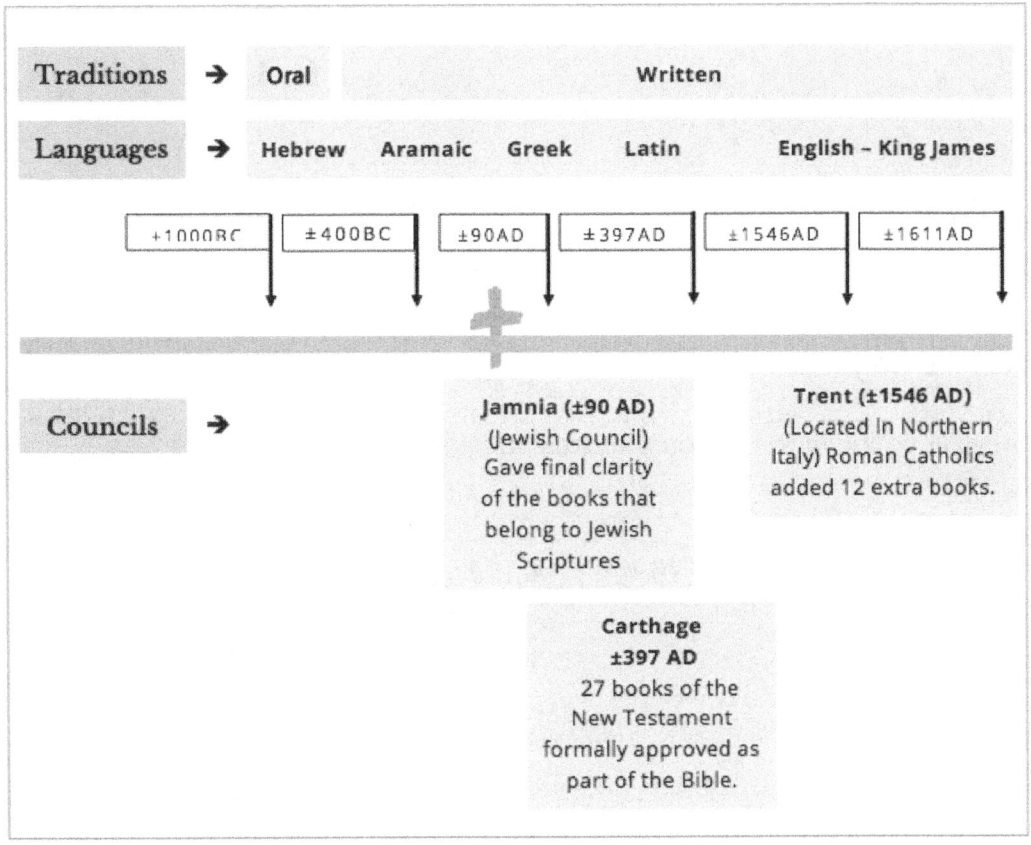

Questions for Group Discussion

- Did the lesson succeed in leaving you in awe of God's Word? Explain!

- What touched you the most in this lesson?

- Is there anything in the lesson that was not clear to you? If so, what was unclear?

- Share blessings and prayer requests and pray for one another.

LESSON 2
OVERVIEW OF THE BIBLE

Purpose
To get an overview of the Bible

Why is it important to have an overview of the Bible?

• It just makes so much more sense if you know where a certain passage fits in the broader biblical story.

The schematic presentation of the overview of the Bible indicates the first nine blocks with a _____ line. This is to show that the Old Testament is building up to a _____ until Jesus appears in the New Testament.

The New Testament (block ten) is not a rising line, because in Jesus, God became human, the personification (fulfillment) of the shadow.
"These are a _____ of the things that were to come; the _____, however, is found in Christ" (Col 2:17 *NIV*). One can conclude that the Old

Testament (covenant) is like a **shadow** pointing to the **person** of Jesus in the New Testament.

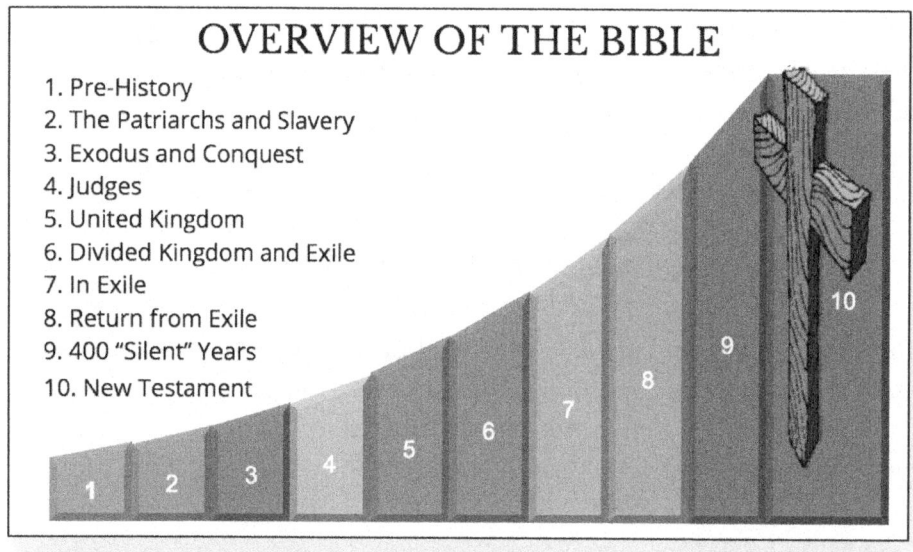

1. Pre-history
(Genesis 1-11)

The events in Genesis 1–11 bear no date and are therefore known as pre-history. Four important events: are being described in these chapters:

1._____

2._____

3._____

4._____

2. Patriarchs and Slavery
(±2000 – ± 1250 BC)
(Genesis 12–50)

The entire Bible is the story of God building a family.

Abraham was the first father of the community.

God forms the new community of believers in such a way that it does not happen naturally but through God's direct intervention.

God does this in two ways.

1. He chooses an old _____ (Abraham's wife, Sarah) as the mother of the community of believers.

2. He calls someone from the _____ to be the father of the new community.

By doing this, God wants us to realize that the community of believers is not the result of human thought and effort. It is the work of a God who wants to be reunited with us.

Genesis ends when Joseph and his family settle in Egypt. The Israelites lived for _____ years in Egypt.

3. Exodus and Conquest

(±1250 – 1220 BC)
(Exodus, Leviticus, Numbers, Deuteronomy and Joshua)

Genesis ends with Joseph and his family in Egypt. Exodus picks up the story _____ years later with a Pharaoh who did not know Joseph and how he had saved the Egyptians from starvation.

God calls Moses to lead the Hebrews out of Egypt into the Promised Land.

God always has a plan! Moses is an unlikely hero:

- _____
- _____
- _____
- _____
- _____
- _____

Conquest of Canaan, the Promised Land

- Moses bids farewell (Deuteronomy)
- Joshua leads the people across the Jordan
- The fall of Jericho
- The land is divided up

4. Judges
(±1200 – ± 1020 BC)
(Judges and Ruth)

The period between the Conquest and Monarchy

The period of the judges covers the events between the entry into the Promised Land and the establishment of the monarchy in Israel.

Tribes not closely united

Judges sent by God to rule

The judges (leaders sent by God) acted timely to restore order in these hostile times.

Well-known Judges and Ruth

The most well-known judges were Othniel, Ehud, Deborah, Gideon, Jephtah and, of course, Samson. The story of Ruth also takes place during the time of Judges.

This was a dark period in the history of Israel.

The book of Judges shows a clear pattern whereby the people would

- _____
- _____ and then again
- _____

5. The United Kingdom

(± 1020 – 925 BC)
1 Samuel, 2 Samuel, 1 Kings 1–11,
1 Chronicles—2 Chronicles 9, Job, Psalms, Proverbs, Ecclesiastes and Song of
Solomon)

The dark time of the Judges paved the way for this period

Samuel warns the people

The three kings of this period

- _____

- _____ and

- _____

6. The Divided Kingdom and Exile

(925 – 586 BC)
(1 Kings 12 – 2 Kings 25, 2 Chronicles 10 – 36, Jonah, Amos, Hosea, Isaiah 1-39,
Micah, Nahum, Zephaniah, Jeremiah, Lamentations, Habakkuk, Obadiah, Isaiah
40-66)

Solomon, a major culprit

"The Lord was very angry with Solomon, for his heart had turned away from
the Lord, the God of Israel, who had appeared to him twice" (1 Kings 11:9, *NLT*).

Solomon treated the southern tribes *(Benjamin and Joseph)* _____
than the northern tribes *(Asher, Dan, Ephraim, Gad, Issachar, Manasseh, Naphtali,
Reuben, Simeon, and Zebulun)*. As a result the ten northern tribes broke away in
925 BC to form an independent kingdom.

The Northern Kingdom retained the name _____, while the
Southern Kingdom became known as _____. Israel had more
territory and wealth, but it was situated on an important trade route and was
therefore exposed to attacks from other nations.

In short, Solomon's disobedience caused the division of the kingdom.

The End of the Northern Kingdom (722 BC)

The _____ Empire was cruel and relentless in war. In 722 BC they
invaded Israel, which had been slowly declining both politically and socially,
and conquered the capital city of Samaria.
The reason why God allowed this to happen is set out in detail in 2 Kings 17:
they continued to sin against God and ignored the warnings of the prophets.

The End of the Southern Kingdom (586 BC)

The Assyrian kingdom collapsed suddenly and unexpectedly in 622 BC when Media and Babylon (modern-day southern Iraq) conquered Nineveh, the capital of Assyria. _____ then became the new world power.

Then, the unthinkable happened:

Jerusalem, the capital of Judah, was invaded and destroyed by Babylon in 586 BC.

The people's persistent _____, despite all the warnings by the prophets, had caused the Lord to allow Jerusalem and the Temple to be destroyed (2 Kings 24:8–25:1).

God's people were then taken to Babylon as exile.

7. In Exile

(597–538 BC)
(Ezekiel and Daniel)

Babylon was the world power during the time God's people were in exile.

Ezekiel and Daniel were prophets in _____.

Way of worship changes.

8. Return from Exile

(538 — 420 BC)
Haggai, Zechariah, Joel, Esther, Ezra, Nehemiah and Malachi

Persian Empire encourages return

The return took place over a long period.

It was during this time that the exiles who returned home were called "Jews" for the first time. This word derives from the Hebrew word Yehudi, which is related to Judah, the tribe into which Jesus was born.

God remains faithful to his promise.

9. 400 "Silent" Years

(420- ±6BC)

Where does the Old Testament end?

Where does the New Testament start?

For 400 years God is 'silent.' There are no prophets, no miracles and no angel visitations. But the silence is broken with the birth of Jesus Christ.

What happened during those 400 years?

The following "décor shifts" occur:

    1. _____ shifts

    2. _____ shifts

    3. _____ shifts

    4. _____ shifts

    5. _____ shifts

1. Political Shifts

The center of world power thus shifted from the east to the west.

Alexander was one of the greatest generals of all time. He subjected the whole inhabited world, including Palestine, to his rule during his short life span.

After his death, his empire was divided among his _____.
They shared Alexander's dream and continued to spread Greek culture, Greek thinking and the Greek language everywhere.

2. Cultural Shifts

The next world rulers, the Romans, **fully _____ the Greek culture**.

The _____ was written in Greek during the first century AD. The Greek culture also had an impact on the Jews in Palestine.

3. Geographical Shifts

During the time of the New Testament, there were probably more Jews in Alexandria than in Jerusalem.

During Roman domination, Palestine (formerly known as Canaan) was divided into three areas; namely,

    1. _____
    2. _____
    3. _____

Previously, Palestine was divided into two areas: Samaria in the north and Judea in the south.

4. Religious Shifts

Alexander the Great's attempts to Hellenize the world led to resistance. New religious parties were formed among the Jews during the 400 silent years in reaction to the pressure to adopt Greek language and ....

- The _____ were known for their rigid adherence to religious prescriptions and traditions of the forefathers.

- The _____ a smaller group than the Pharisees, were politically more active.

- Strictly speaking, _____ were not a party but a group of laymen who studied the Law of Moses.

- The _____ were followers of the Pharisees' faith but were firmly set against domination by the Romans. They tried to get rid of Roman rule.

5. Language Shifts

The language of the inhabitants of Palestine changed from Hebrew to _____ (a language related to Hebrew) after the period of exile in Babylonia. Hebrew was mainly the language of the _____.

During the time of Jesus, the priests and rabbis only used Hebrew for religious matters. Latin was spoken in Rome, but _____ was spoken in the rest of the Roman Empire. His disciples spoke Aramaic.

10. The New Testament

When God raised the curtain after the 400 silent years, the world was prepared for the rapid spread of the _____.

- There was now a world language (koine Greek),
- It was easy to travel
- Jewish settlements and synagogues were present everywhere.

The silent years ended with the birth of Christ.

The 27 books that make up the New Testament were nearly all written before the end of AD 100.

The 27 books can be grouped the following way:

• The four Gospels, which describe the life of Jesus from different perspectives

1. _____
2. _____
3. _____
4. _____

• The first years of the Christian Church

The Acts of the Apostles

• The letters of Paul

Romans, 1 and 2 Corinthians, Galatians, Ephesians, Philippians, Colossians, 1 and 2 Thessalonians, 1 and 2 Timothy, Titus and Philemon

• The general letters

Hebrews, James, 1 and 2 Peter, 1–3 John and Jude)

• John's visions

Revelation

Questions for Group Discussion

- Did the material succeed in giving you an overview of God's Word?

- What touched you the most in the lesson?

- Was there anything surprising in this week's material? If so, how were you surprised?

- Share blessings and prayer requests and pray for one another.

LESSON 3
TYPE OF LITERATURE

Purpose
To determine the different types of literature

Why is it important to have an understanding of the literature of the Bible?

- to realize that the different types of literature are each being read in a different way.

The Bible was written by approximately _____ authors over a period of more than 1500 years.

The author's (sender's) goal was to communicate the _____ in their hearts with others (recipients) by writing them down.

They used different _____ (genres) to write down their message.

The different forms of writing are known as literature. The word literature literally means "things made of letters".

SENDER

MEANING

FORM

RECIPIENT

Literature can be classified into two main **TECHNIQUES**: _____ & _____.

Prose is the most _____ form of language. The English word 'prose' is derived from the Latin prōsa, which literally translates as 'straight-forward.' Because of this, prose is observed in many areas of writing, most especially in newspapers, magazines, and even encyclopedias.

Poetry (from the Latin poeta, a poet) is typically reserved for _____ something special in an artistic way.

The Bible is a _____ of types of literature. God's message of love is written in different types of literature.

The **MEANING** is written in many _____ such as Narratives, the Law, Prophecy, Wisdom and Epistles.

PROSE	POETRY
Narrative/History The Law Prophecy Gospel Epistle (Letter) Apocalyptic Writing	Wisdom Psalms Prophecy

Hebrew poetry typically was not based on rhyme, but on a concept known as
_____. It means that there is a connection between two
successive lines. Instead of rhyming words, as our poetry does, the Hebrews
rhymed _____.

There are basically **three** primary types of parallelism:

    1. _____

    2. _____

    3. _____

The Reason for Parallelisms

    1. It creates _____.

    2. It highlights the _____.

    3. It involves your _____.

    4. It stimulates your _____.

Synonymous Parallelism	Antithetic Parallelism	Synthetic Parallelism
The second line _____ the thought of the first line in different words (Most popular in prophets).	The second line _____ with the first, expressing the opposite thought. These are most common in Proverbs and Psalms.	The second line (or following lines) _____ on the thought of the first line and adds something fresh.
EXAMPLE Isaiah 53:5	**EXAMPLE** Proverbs 10:1	**EXAMPLE** Isaiah 60:5
"But he was pierced *for our transgressions,* he was crushed *for our iniquities."* (NIV)	"A wise son *brings joy to his father,* but a foolish son *brings grief to his mother."* (NIV)	"Then you will look and be radiant, your heart will throb and swell with joy; the wealth on the seas will be brought to you," (NIV)

Match the corresponding letter with the respective parallelism

Synonymous parallelism
match _____

A

"Deliverers will go up on Mount Zion to govern the mountains of Esau. And the kingdom will be the Lord's."   *Obadiah 21 (NIV)*

Antithetic parallelism
match _____

B

"I will turn your religious festivals into mourning and all your singing into weeping."
                    Amos 8:10 (NIV)

Synthetic parallelism
match _____

C

"The poor plead for mercy,
but the rich answer harshly."
                    Proverbs 18:23 (NIV)

Read the following two passages

Exodus 14:1-9

1 Then the Lord said to Moses,
2 "Tell the Israelites to turn back and encamp near Pi Hahiroth, between Migdol and the sea. They are to encamp by the sea, directly opposite Baal Zephon.
3 Pharaoh will think, 'The Israelites are wandering around the land in confusion, hemmed in by the desert.'
4 And I will harden Pharaoh's heart, and he will pursue them. But I will gain glory for myself through Pharaoh and all his army, and the Egyptians will know that I am the Lord." So the Israelites did this.
5 When the king of Egypt was told that the people had fled, Pharaoh and his officials changed their minds about them and said, "What have we done? We have let the Israelites go and have lost their services!" 6 So he had his chariot made ready and took his army with him.
7 He took six hundred of the best chariots, along with all the other chariots of Egypt, with officers over all of them.
8 The Lord hardened the heart of Pharaoh king of Egypt, so that he pursued the Israelites, who were marching out boldly.
9 The Egyptians—all Pharaoh's horses and chariots, horsemen and troops—pursued the Israelites and overtook them as they camped by the sea near Pi Hahiroth, opposite Baal Zephon. (NIV)

Exodus 15:1-6

1 Then Moses and the Israelites sang this song to the Lord:
"I will sing to the Lord,
  for he is highly exalted.
Both horse and driver
  he has hurled into the sea.
2 "The Lord is my strength and my defense;
  he has become my salvation.
He is my God, and I will praise him,
  my father's God, and I will exalt him.
3 The Lord is a warrior;
  the Lord is his name.
4 Pharaoh's chariots and his army
  he has hurled into the sea.
The best of Pharaoh's officers
  are drowned in the Red Sea.
5 The deep waters have covered them;
  they sank to the depths like a stone.
6 Your right hand, Lord,
  was majestic in power.
Your right hand, Lord,
  shattered the enemy. (NIV)

What have you noticed?

- Both passages deal with the same event when the Lord delivered the Israelites from the Egyptians.

- The first passage is in _____, and the second one is in _____.

- The same message can be written in both prose and poetry.

SUMMARY OF BIBLICAL GENRES

- **Narratives / History (Prose)**

Genesis and the first half of **Exodus***,* **Numbers***,* **Joshua***,* **Judges***,* **Ruth***, 1 and 2* **Samuel***, 1 and 2* **Kings***, 1 and 2* **Chronicles***,* **Ezra***,* **Nehemiah***,* **Esther***,* **Jonah***, and possibly* **Acts**

This is the most _____ genre.

- **Law (Prose)**

The last half of **Exodus***; also* **Leviticus***,* **Deuteronomy**

These include laws that prohibited things but also encouraged actions / deeds. The most famous laws in the Bible are the _____ (Exodus 20 and Deuteronomy 5).

- **Wisdom (Poetry)**
Wisdom literature focuses on questions about the _____ of life. They are collections of wise sayings meant to _____ the moral and ethical lives of their readers.

- **Psalms**
The Book of Psalms is for the most part a book of _____ and _____.

- **Prophecy (Prose and Poetry)**

The prophetic genre deals with the words of the prophets. While narratives describe events, prophecies proclaim the message of God. A prophet is God's _____.

A prophecy's primary focus is to call on people to _____.

- **Gospel (Prose)**

"Gospel" means "_____" and refers to the first four books of the New Testament.

- **Epistle / Letters (Prose)**

The letters refer to the _____ letters of the New Testament.

- **Apocalyptic Writing (Prose)**

"Apocalypse" is a Greek word meaning "_____", "a revealing or unfolding of things that previously were not known".

A characteristic of apocalyptic literature is the use of images, symbols and symbolic numbers. John's visions in Revelation and Daniel 7-12 are examples of apocalyptic writing.

A Schematic Presentation of the Biblical Genres

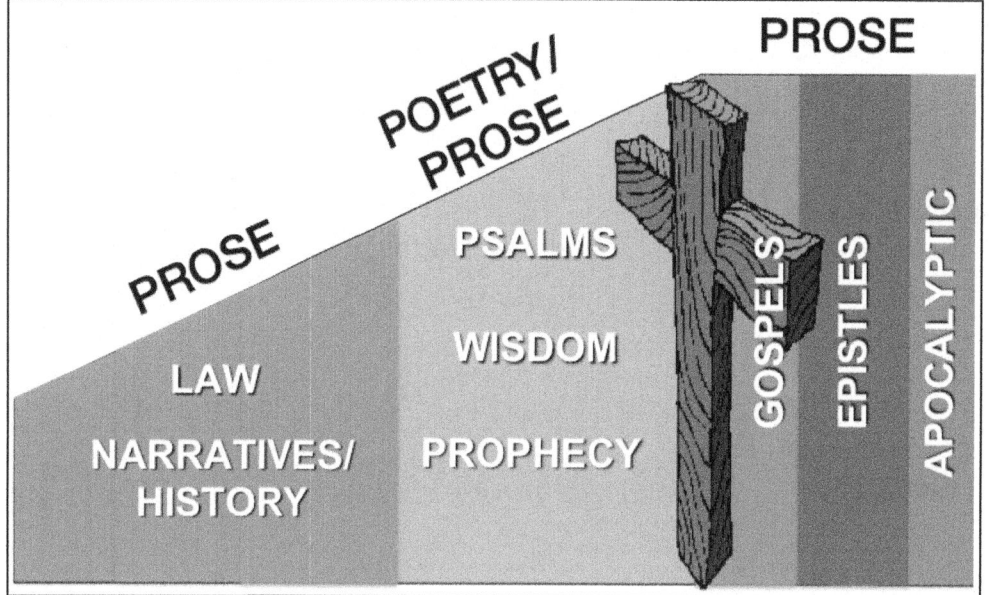

Match the corresponding letter to the type of literature

Narrative match

_____

Law match

_____

Wisdom match

_____

Poetry match

_____

Prophecy match

_____

Gospel match

_____

Epistle match

_____

Apocalyptic match

_____

(Answers are on page 44)

A

[1] And I saw an angel coming down out of heaven, having the key to the Abyss and holding in his hand a great chain. [2] He seized the dragon, that ancient serpent, who is the devil, or Satan, and bound him for a thousand years.   *(Rev 20 NIV)*

E

[6] The wolf will live with the lamb, the leopard will lie down with the goat, the calf and the lion and the yearling together; and a little child will lead them.

(Is 11 NIV)

B

[16] For God so loved the world that he gave his one and only Son, that whoever believes in him shall not perish but have eternal life.   *(John 3 NIV)*

F

[22] For it is written that Abraham had two sons, one by the slave woman and the other by the free woman. [23] His son by the slave woman was born according to the flesh, but his son by the free woman was born as the result of a divine promise.

(Gal 4 NIV)

C

[3] "You shall have no other gods before me. [4] "You shall not make for yourself an image in the form of anything in heaven above or on the earth beneath or in the waters below.   *(Ex 20 NIV)*

G

[5] Trust in the Lord with all your heart and lean not on your own understanding;
[6] in all your ways submit to him,
and he will make your paths straight.
[7] Do not be wise in your own eyes;
fear the Lord and shun evil.

(Prov 3 NIV)

D

[6] Now Joseph was well-built and handsome, [7] and after a while his master's wife took notice of Joseph and said, "Come to bed with me!" [8] But he refused. "With me in charge," he told her, "my master does not concern himself with anything in the house; everything he owns he has entrusted to my care.

(Gen 39 NIV)

H

[1] The Lord is my shepherd,
I lack nothing.
[2] He makes me lie down in green pastures,
he leads me beside quiet waters,
[3] he refreshes my soul.
He guides me along the right paths for his name's sake

(Psalm 23 NIV)

Questions for Group Discussion

- Why is it important to identify the different kinds of literature of the Bible?

- Name the two techniques in which literature can be divided?

- What touched you the most in the lesson?

- Is there anything in the lesson that was not clear to you? If so, what was unclear?

- Share blessings and prayer requests and pray for one another

Answers to questions on page 42.

Narrative match **D**

Law match **C**

Wisdom match **G**

Poetry match **H**

Prophecy match **E**

Gospel match **B**

Epistles match **F**

Apocalyptic match **A**

LESSON 4
THE GPS-METHOD

Purpose
To master the GPS-Method

It is not always easy to understand the Bible.

The reason is that between us in the 21st century and the people of the Bible there are many _____. There are differences of

- _____
- _____
- _____
- _____
- _____

The original receivers (first readers) best understood the Bible. Let us illustrate it with Romans 12:20.

> **"If your enemy is hungry, feed him; If he is thirsty, give him a drink; For in so doing you will heap coals of fire on his head."**
>
> *New King James Version*

> **"If your enemies are hungry, feed them; if they are thirsty, give them a drink; for by doing this you will make them burn with shame."**
>
> *Good News Bible*

It is clear that the Good News Bible conveys the _____ as the original receivers understood it.
To the original receivers "heap coals of fire on his head" was an _____ _____ meaning "to burn with shame".

How can the message to the original receivers speak to us in the 21ˢᵗ century?

We follow _____ processes which we call the Bible GPS (**G**od **P**ositioning **S**ystem).

It includes the processes of

- _____

- _____

- _____

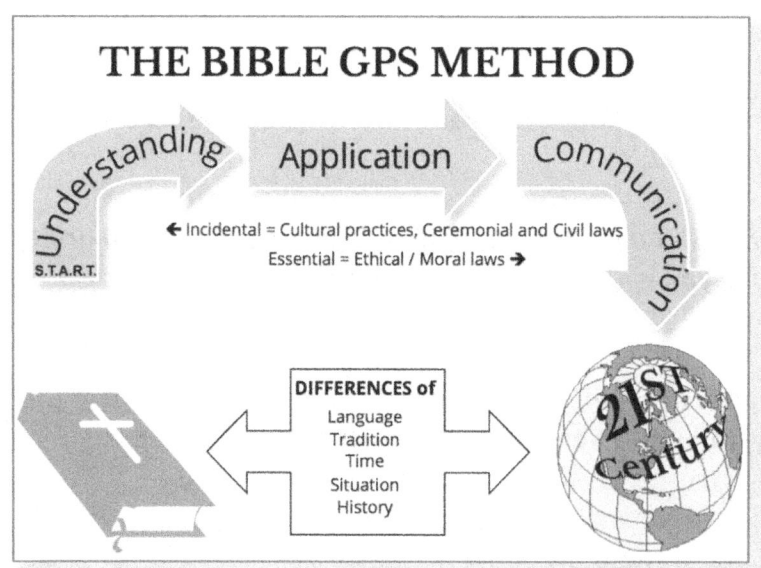

The **Goal** of the process of **UNDERSTANDING** is to understand the message as well as or almost as well as the _____ receivers did.

The Process of UNDERSTANDING consists of _____ steps. These steps form the acronym _____.

    P **1.** **Situation**

    R **2.** **Type of Literature**

    A
    Y **3.** **Analysis the passage**

    E **4.** **Relationship to the rest of the Bible**

    R **5.** **Test of your finding**

We do this process prayerfully under the guidance of God's Spirit.

A. THE PROCESS OF UNDERSTANDING

Let us apply the process of UNDERSTANDING to **Ephesians 2: 1-10** (page 53)

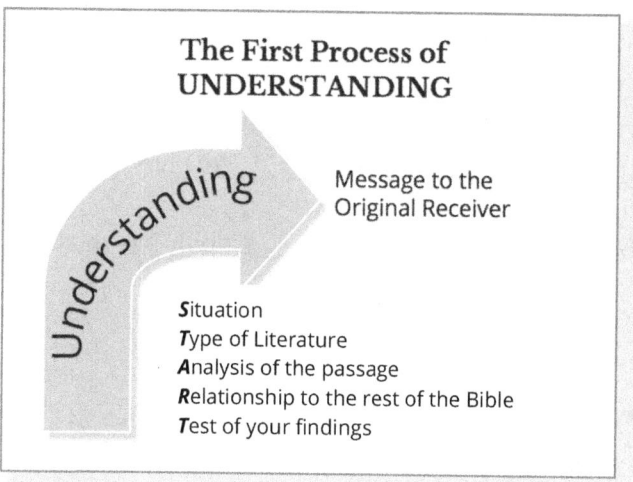

The First Process of
UNDERSTANDING

Understanding

Message to the
Original Receiver

Situation
Type of Literature
Analysis of the passage
Relationship to the rest of the Bible
Test of your findings

- **The FIRST step of understanding: Ephesians 2:1-10**

1. Situation

The situation or context of a passage will help you better understand the text. Think of a teacher who was very surprised when one of her top students failed. Once the student explained to his teacher that his father had passed away the night before the exam, the teacher understood why her top student did not perform well.

You understand a passage much better if you have insight into the circumstances in which the text was written.

How can we get a better understanding of the situation?

You get a better understanding of the situation by asking the following questions:

- **Who was the Sender (Author) and Receiver (Reader)?**

Paul wrote the letter from prison (Ephesians 3:1, 4:1, 6:20) to the believers in Ephesus and Asia Minor.

- **Where does the passage fit in the structure (division) of the book and Bible?**

Study Bibles often gives a complete description of a Biblical book. Ephesians is part of the Epistles of the New Testament.

- **What was the purpose of the letter?**

To remind the believers what a privilege it is to be part of the body of Christ as a Jew and a non-Jew.

- **What was the political situation?**

Rome was the world power and they allowed the Jews to practice their religion across the Roman Empire.

- **What was the cultural background?**

The Greek culture flourished. Greek was the common language.

- **What was the economic background?**

Ephesus was very strategically located, and was as major a port city as Alexandria in Egypt and Antioch in Syria. It is located to the west of Asia Minor (where Turkey is today) and was on the main route between Rome and the East.

- **What was the religious background?**

At that time there was a religious heresy called "Gnosticism". "Gnosticism" comes from the Greek word "gnosis" which means "knowledge". Gnosticism teaches that salvation is reached through special knowledge (gnosis) of a Supreme Being. They make a clear separation between the material and spiritual world. According to them, the visible (material) does not have an effect on your mind. So they continued to live immorally and still believed that they were spiritually pure.

Where can you get all the information?

- Study Bibles
- Bible commentaries
- Internet (http://www.biblestudytools.com/ephesians/)
- Your church

- **The SECOND step of understanding: Ephesians 2:1-10**

2. Type of Literature

It is important to determine what kind of literature the passage is. You can not, for example, read a poem as a story is read (see page 33).

Paul's message is in the FORM (genre) of a LETTER.

- **The THIRD step of understanding: Ephesians 2:1-10**

3. Analysis of the passage

This is where we spend the most time.

The following steps will help you to read the letters of the New Testament.

3.1 Write out the passage into _____

Because what the writers wrote was very compact and loaded, I have broken the verses into smaller sections (see page 65).

It is easier to understand directions to someone's house if the steps are written like a list rather than in sentences. It just makes it easier to read.

3.2 Mark the main _____ (zoom in)

How do we mark the main themes? You first **zoom in** to the passage by marking everything that relates.

Hint

- You can use colored pens to mark words. You can also use a pen or pencil to mark words with triangles, squares, circles or ticks or anything else that is noticeable. This is called **meaning indicators**.

- Indicate at the beginning of each verse an "**E**" for explanation and an "**I**" for instruction. It helps us to see how the author developed his thoughts. (You will notice that this section is not instructional at all.

Exercise

Let us **zoom in** to Ephesians 2:1-10. Go to page 53.

Mark all the negative words and phrases in verses 1-3 with the same meaning indicator *(See Introduction 1, page 3)*.

Mark all the positive words in verses 4-9 with a different meaning indicator *(See Introduction, page 4)*.

In verse 10 the focus switches back to humanity's responsibility.
Mark everything people need to do in verse 10 with a different meaning indicator *(See Introduction, page 4)*.

Ephesians 2: 1-10

¹ As for you,
you were **dead** in your **transgressions** and **sins**,
² in which you used to live
when you **followed the ways of this world**
and of the **ruler of the kingdom of the air**,
the spirit who is **now at work**
in those who are **disobedient**.
³All of us also lived among them at one time,
gratifying the **cravings** of our **sinful nature**
and **following** its **desires** and **thoughts**.
Like the rest, we were by nature **objects of wrath**.
⁴ But because of his great love for us,
God, who is rich in mercy,
⁵ made us alive with Christ
even when we were dead in transgressions–
it is by grace you have been saved.
⁶ And God raised us up with Christ
and seated us with him
in the heavenly realms in Christ Jesus,
⁷ in order that in the coming ages
he might show the incomparable riches of his grace,
expressed in his kindness to us in Christ Jesus.
⁸ For it is by grace you have been saved,
through faith–and this not from yourselves,
it is the gift of God–
⁹ not by works,
so that no one can boast.
¹⁰ For we are God's workmanship,
created in Christ Jesus to do good works,
which God prepared in advance for us to do. (NIV)

3.3 Explain difficult words and phrases (if necessary)

This section does not really have difficult words. It does have words that are loaded with rich meaning like "grace."

3.4 Summarize the main sections in your own words (zoom out)

After you have marked Ephesians 2:1-10, you **zoom out** to see how the author had arranged his thoughts.

- **Verses 1-3**: Paul uses many words which refer to a big mess (e.g., transgressions, sin and wrath).
  Try to summarise verses 1-3 in one short sentence or one word next to verses 1-3 on page 53.

- **Verses 4-9**: The word "but" in verse 4 brings a twist in Paul's thought. These verses are about God's goodness.
  Try to summarise verses 4-9 in one short sentence or one word next to verses 4-9 on page 53.

- **Verse 10**: Here the focus shifts back to humanity's responsibility to do good works because we are thankful for God's grace.
  Try to summarise verse 10 in one short sentence or one word next to the verse 10 on page 53.

In light of the findings of the previous three steps, we now attempt to see how the author arranged the main themes.

- **Verses 1-3**: What a _____ (sin or guilt)

- **Verses 4-9**: What a _____ (salvation or grace)

- **Verse 10**: What a _____ (service or gratitude)

3.5 Conclude and summarize the message to the original receiver

I am saved, not by works, but by faith in Christ. I do good works because I am thankful for what God has done for me (and still does) in Christ.

- **The FOURTH step of understanding: Ephesians 2:1-10**

4. Relationship to the rest of the bible

In this step we determine whether the findings of the previous step (message to the original receiver) relate to the rest of the Bible. If the result of your analysis is that you do not always have to forgive, then you will soon realize that other passages do not proclaim this message. This means that you haven't interpreted the passage correctly.

- **The FITH step of understanding: Ephesians 2:1-10**

5. Test of your findings

In this step you test your findings (Biblical interpretation) against those of others (e.g. commentaries and study Bibles). Many others before you have wrestled with this passage. Reading the interpretations of others, will confirm that you understood this passage correctly or that you are off track.

B. THE PROCESS OF APPLICATION

We have seen that the process of **UNDERSTANDING** helps us to determine the message to the original receiver.

The following process, **APPLICATION**, helps us to determine whether or not the message to the original recipient is still applicable to us in the 21st century.

It is clear that we do not follow all the instructions of the Bible anymore. We still believe that we should honor our parents (Leviticus 19: 3), yet we don't believe we should wear clothes only made of one textile (Leviticus 19:19).

How do you determine when the message to the original recipient still applies to us?

You need to distinguish the difference between an _____ and an _____.

An Incidental (Relative)
The message is only applicable to the original receiver

An Essential (Absolute)
The message is applicable to the original receiver and the people of the 21st century

How do you determine when the message to the original receiver is applicable (essential) to us, or not (incidental)?

A good place to start is to distinguish the different laws in the Bible as well as cultural practices. (The author is totally aware that not all church traditions agree on this distinction.)

The Different Laws and Cultural Practices

Civil Laws	Ceremonial Laws	Cultural Practices	Moral Law

PURPOSE

Civil Laws	Ceremonial Laws	Cultural Practices	Moral Law
Regulating the nation of Israel	Animal sacrifices to make atonement for sin. Point to Christ, the true Lamb	Comprise the ways people do certain things	Universal guidelines telling us how to live

EXAMPLE

Civil Laws	Ceremonial Laws	Cultural Practices	Moral Law
Building regulations *(Deut 22:8)*	The Passover *(Lev 16)*	To greet with a kiss. (1 Peter 5:14)	The Ten Commandments *(Ex 20)*

Civil (Judicial) Laws were _____ to the original receivers but are _____ to us because our situation is different.

Ceremonial (Ritual) Laws were _____ to the original receivers but are _____ to us because it was fulfilled in Christ's offering on the cross.

Cultural practices were _____L to the original receivers but are _____ to us because our culture, time, situation and history are different.

Behind every civil and ceremonial law is a moral law (a commandment of love). We do not need to bring sacrifices of lambs to the temple anymore. Our whole life is now a living sacrifice to God (Romans 12:1). Those passages, especially the ceremonial laws, will help us better understand and appreciate the sacrifice of Christ.

Moral (Ethical) Laws were _____ to the original receiver and are also _____ to us because they go beyond language, culture, time, situation and history.

It is very important to distinguish between an **INCIDENTAL** and an **ESSENTIAL** message. The danger is to interpret an Essential as an Incidental or to interpret an Incidental as an Essential.

An illustration of the importance of this process: LEGALISM versus "ANYTHING GOES"

The danger when an **INCIDENTAL** is being perceived as an **ESSENTIAL**

INCIDENTAL		ESSENTIAL		
INCIDENTAL The message is only applicable to the original receiver.	perceived as	**ESSENTIAL** The message is applicable to the original receiver and people of the 21st century	=	_____

Example

INCIDENTAL		ESSENTIAL		
INCIDENTAL Kiss as a way to greet. (1 Pet 5:14).	perceived as	**ESSENTIAL** Christians shall kiss one another.	=	_____

The danger when an **ESSENTIAL** is being perceived as an **INCIDENTAL**

| **ESSENTIAL** The message is applicable to the original receiver and people of the 21st century. | perceived as | **INCIDENTAL** The message is only applicable to the original receiver. | = | " _____ _____ " |

Example

| **ESSENTIAL** Jesus is GOD. (John 20:28) | perceived as | **INCIDENTAL** Jesus was only a good moral teacher. | = | " _____ _____ " |

Determine whether the following passages are applicable (essential) or not applicable (incidental) to us.

Check the right answer:

Exodus 20:12-16

[12] Honor your father and your mother, so that your days may be long in the land that the Lord your God is giving you.

[13] You shall not murder.

[14] You shall not commit adultery.

[15] You shall not steal.

[16] You shall not bear false witness against your neighbor. (NRSV)

Applicable _____
Not Applicable _____

Leviticus 11:4

But among those that chew the cud or have divided hoofs, you shall not eat the following: the camel, for even though it chews the cud, it does not have divided hoofs; it is unclean for you. (NRSV)

Applicable _____
Not Applicable _____

Psalm 100:1-12

[1] Make a joyful noise to the Lord,
 all the earth.

[2] Worship the Lord with gladness;
 come into his presence with singing. (NRSV)

Applicable ....
Not Applicable ....

Deuteronomy 22:11
You shall not wear clothes made of wool and linen woven together. (NRSV)

Applicable _____
Not Applicable _____

James 4: 11
Do not speak evil against one another, brothers and sisters. Whoever speaks evil against another or judges another, speaks evil against the law and judges the law; but if you judge the law, you are not a doer of the law but a judge.
(NRSV)

Applicable _____
Not Applicable _____

1 Corinthians 11:6
For if a woman will not veil herself, then she should cut off her hair; but if it is disgraceful for a woman to have her hair cut off or to be shaved, she should wear a veil. (NRSV)

Applicable _____
Not Applicable _____

Exodus 29:22
You shall take the ram of ordination, and boil its flesh in a holy place; (NRSV)

Applicable _____
Not Applicable _____

Exodus 21:16-17
[16] Whoever kidnaps a person, whether that person has been sold or is still held in possession, shall be put to death.
[17] Whoever curses father or mother shall be put to death. (NRSV)

Applicable _____
Not Applicable _____

Matthew 6:25

"Therefore I tell you, do not worry about your life, what you will eat or what you will drink," (NRSV)

Applicable _____
Not Applicable _____

Romans 16:16

Greet one another with a holy kiss. All the churches of Christ greet you. (NRSV)

Applicable _____
Not Applicable _____

John 13:34-35

[34] I give you a new commandment, that you love one another. Just as I have loved you, you also should love one another. [35] By this everyone will know that you are my disciples, if you have love for one another. (NRSV)

Applicable _____
Not Applicable _____

Genesis 22:2

"Take your son, your only son Isaac, whom you love, and go to the land of Moriah, and offer him there as a burnt offering on one of the mountains that I shall show you." (NRSV)

Applicable _____
Not Applicable _____

1 Thessalonians 5:16-18

[16] Rejoice always, [17] pray without ceasing, [18] give thanks in all circumstances; for this is the will of God in Christ Jesus for you. (NRSV)

Applicable _____
Not Applicable _____

C. THE PROCESSES OF COMMUNICATION

In the next process, **COMMUNICATION**, we use creative ways to communicate the _____ in the 21st century.

We do this through preaching, drama, art, PowerPoint presentations, puppetry, videos and more. Your life must also communicate the message!

Conclusion

Why are there so many translations of the Bible?

1. The _____ change

We no longer speak the same language that people spoke generations ago. God wants to communicate with us through his Word and therefore it is only logical that one reads the Bible in a language that is easily understandable.

2. Translation _____ differ

There are basically three translation techniques.

1) _____ **translations**
   (King James Version)

Direct translations translate the _____ of the writer directly. The Hebrew and Greek texts are simply replaced with English words.

2) _____ **translations**
   (Good News Translation & the New International Version)

Dynamic translations seek to bring across more accurately the _____. The New International Version will therefore adjust the idioms in order to convey the meaning (see diagram).

The dynamic translation uses shorter sentences and simpler and more modern words.

3) _____
   (Living Bible)

The Paraphrase is not really a translation. This is actually a _____, a description. It writes in a more informal language about what the original text says and conveys the meaning as well as the feeling. It almost reads like a story book.

Romans 12:20 as illustration

DIRECT TRANSLATION (Word-for-word) King James Version	DYNAMIC TRANSLATION (Meaning) Good News Translation	PARAPHRASE (Retelling) Living Bible
"Therefore if thine enemy hunger, feed him; if he thirst, give him drink: for in so doing thou shalt heap coals of fire on his head."	"If your enemies are hungry, feed them; if they are thirsty, give them a drink; for by doing this you will make them burn with shame."	"Instead, feed your enemy if he is hungry. If he is thirsty give him something to drink and you will be "heaping coals of fire on his head." In other words, he will feel ashamed of himself for what he has done to you."

Questions for Group Discussion

- Did the lesson help you to master the processes of Understanding, Application and Communication?

- Why is it important to distinguish between an ESSENTIAL and a RELATIVE message?

- What touched you the most in the lesson?

- Is there anything in the lesson that was not clear to you? If so, what was unclear?

- Share blessings and prayer requests and pray for one another.

LESSON 5
THE EPISTLES / LETTERS

Purpose
To get a better understanding of the Epistles

Introductory Remarks

The Epistles are letters written to the fledgling churches and individual believers in the earliest days of Christianity.

These letters addressed specific contexts (like letters), but none of them was intended to be kept private or confidential. All twenty-one books are public documents linked to particular audiences and particular occasions.

The Epistles include _____ of the New Testament's 27 books, extending from Romans to Jude.

The apostle Paul wrote _____ of these Epistles:
Romans, 1 and 2 Corinthians, Galatians, Ephesians, Philippians, Colossians, 1 and 2 Thessalonians, 1 and 2 Timothy, Titus, and Philemon.

These Epistles are known as _____ **Epistles.**

Within the Pauline Epistles there are two subgroups:

- _____ *Epistles* (Ephesians, Philippians, Colossians, and Philemon) because they were written during Paul's two-year house arrest in Rome (Acts 28:30–31).

- _____ *Epistles* (1 and 2 Timothy and Titus) which were written to church leaders and include many teachings regarding practices within the early church.

Following the Pauline Epistles are eight _____ **Epistles** (since they were written to a "universal" audience) which includes Hebrews, James, 1 and 2 Peter, 1, 2, and 3 John, and Jude.

Following the Pauline Epistles are eight _____ **Epistles** (since they were written to a "universal" audience) which includes Hebrews, James, 1 and 2 Peter, 1, 2, and 3 John, and Jude.

- The author of **Hebrews** is unknown (though many have historically attributed it to Paul or one of Paul's associates).

- **James** was one of the earliest New Testament writings and was written by James, the brother of Jesus (1 Corinthians 15:7).

- The apostle **Peter** wrote 1 and 2 Peter.

- The apostle **John** (the same author of the Gospel of John and Revelation) wrote 1 John, 2 John, and 3 John.

- **Jude**, another brother of Jesus, wrote the short Epistle of Jude (Jude 1:1).[1]

1. https://www.gotquestions.org/what-is-an-epistle.html

The Pauline Epistles

- o Romans
- o 1 & 2 Corinthians
- o Galatians
- o Ephesians (Prison Epistle)
- o Philippians (Prison Epistle)
- o Colossians (Prison Epistle)
- o 1 & 2 Thessalonians
- o 1 & 2 Timothy (Pastoral Epistle)
- o Titus (Pastoral Epistle)
- o Philemon (Prison Epistle)

The General Epistles

- o Hebrews
- o James
- o 1 & 2 Peter
- o 1 - 3 John
- o Jude

The Nature of Epistles

1. The Epistles are not a homogeneous lot

Romans and Philemon, for example, differ from one another not only in _____ but also to the degree that one is far more personal than the other.

The Epistles also differ in _____. The following list explains the various elements that you would expect to find in an ancient letter.

a) The name of the writer. (e.g., Paul, Peter, etc.).
b) The name of the recipient (e.g., the church of God at Corinth).
c) A greeting (e.g., "Grace and peace to you from God our Father...").
d) A prayer wish or thanksgiving (e.g., "I always give thanks for you...").
e) The body - containing an argument, answering questions, giving instructions, etc.).
f) Final greeting and farewell (e.g., "The grace of the Lord Jesus Christ be with you...").

Not all of the letters in the New Testament follow this pattern. Some have various elements missing; so don't think that they all must be there.

d), for example, is completely missing in Galatians, 1 Timothy and Titus, whereas in 2 Corinthians, Ephesians and 1 Peter this thanksgiving turns into a doxology (praise). James and 2 Peter also miss the final greeting and farewell. 1 John has none of the formal elements of a letter.[1]

---

1. Gordon D. Fee & Douglas Stuart, *How to Read the Bible For All Its Worth,* 2nd edn. (Grand Rapids: Zondervan, 1993), 50-53

2. Epistles are occasional documents

Although they are not a homogeneous group, there is one thing that all of the Epistles have in common: they are all arising out of and intended for a *specific* _____, and they are from the *first century*; e.g. Paul talking to Philemon about Onesimus (a runaway slave).[1]

1. Gordon D. Fee & Douglas Stuart, *How to Read the Bible For All Its Worth,* 2nd edn. (Grand Rapids: Zondervan, 1993), 50-53

The Historical Context
(Background)

- **Consult a _____ dictionary or a commentary.**

- **Read the whole letter in _____ to get the big picture of the letter.**

It is recommended to jot down the answers to the following questions:

1) What do you notice about the people the letter is written to? (Were they Jews or Greeks, wealthy or slave, and what were their their problems and attitudes?)

2) What is the author's attitude?

3) Are their any specific things mentioned about why the letter was written (the occasion)?

4) Write down the letter's natural, logical divisions. It is easier to study or read a letter in convenient "packages."[1]

---

1. Gordon D. Fee & Douglas Stuart, *How to Read the Bible For All Its Worth,* 2nd edn. (Grand Rapids: Zondervan, 1993), 53-54

Using Philippians, the answers to the questions are:

1. The recipients of this letter were the church in Philippi, one of the leading cities in the district of Macedonia (Greece). The city of Philippi was named after King Philip II of Macedon, father of Alexander the Great. It was a prosperous city.[1]

2. Paul was a prisoner when he wrote this letter to thank the Philippians for the gift they had sent him upon learning of his detention at Rome (1:5; 4:10–19). This letter stands out as one of the most personal that Paul wrote. It is joyful in nature and doesn't harshly rebuke the congregation.

3. The apostle Paul did not write Philippians in response to a crisis, as he did with Galatians and Colossians. Instead, he wrote this letter to express his appreciation for the material support for his ministry (2 Corinthians 8:11; Philippians 4:15–18). Paul's affection for these people is clear throughout the letter as he encouraged them to live out their faith in joy and unity (1:3–5, 25–26; 4:1).[2]

4. The principal divisions of the Letter to the Philippians are the following:

   - Greetings (1:1–2)
   - Thanksgiving and Prayer for the Philippians (1:3–11)
   - Paul's Personal Circumstances (1:12–26)
   - Exhortations (1:27–2:18)
   - Paul's Associates in the Gospel (2:19–30)
   - Warnings against Judaizers and Antinomians (3:1–4:1)
   - Final Exhortations, Thanks and Conclusion (4:2–23)[3]

1. https://www.biblica.com/bible/online-bible/scholar-notes/niv-study-bible/intro-to-philippians/
2. Chuck Swindoll, https://www.insight.org/resources/bible/the-pauline-epistles/philippians
3. https://www.biblica.com/bible/online-bible/scholar-notes/niv-study-bible/intro-to-philippians/

The Literary Context
(What's being said)

When reading the Epistles it is very important to think not verses, but

_____.

Focusing on paragraphs makes it easier to trace the arguments as answers to the problems being addressed.

Assignment

Find a quiet place this week and read the whole letter from your Bible in one sitting to get the big picture of the letter to the Philippians.

How the Epistles apply to us today?

To answer the questions in how the Epistles apply to us, we must first look at God's Word to the original receivers before we examine his Word to us.

We determine this in the Process of _____ (START); the first step of the GPS method. The Process of Understanding helps us to determine what was God's word to the original receivers.

The second Process of _____ helps us to determine whether the message to the original receivers is applicable (essential) or not (incidental) to us in the 21st century.

Guidelines to determine whether the message is applicable or not

- Remember the Basic Rule: A text cannot mean something to us that it could not have meant to its ....[1]

- When we share a .... life situation with a first century situation, God's Word to us is the same as it was to them.[2]

- When our situation and that of the original recipients is different, look for the ....principle behind what is being said.

- A scripture's context will help you decide whether a verse has a direct or indirect application for today.

Conclusion

"To answer the questions how the Epistles apply to us, we must look at God's Word to the **original receivers** before we examine God's Word to _____.[3]

1. Gordon D. Fee & Douglas Stuart, *How to Read the Bible For All Its Worth,* 2nd edn. (Grand Rapids: Zondervan, 1993), 69-70
2. Gordon D. Fee & Douglas Stuart, *How to Read the Bible For All Its Worth,* 2nd edn. (Grand Rapids: Zondervan, 1993), 70-71
3. Siôn Glaze, http://admin.cmf.org.uk/pdf/nucleus/NUEaster09/NUeaster09-38-39.pdf, 2009

Questions for Group Discussion

- Did the lesson help you to get a better understanding of the Epistles?

- What touched you the most in the lesson?

- Is there anything in the lesson that was not clear to you? If so, what was unclear?

- Share blessings and prayer requests and pray for one another.

LESSON 6
THE GPS-METHOD APPLIED TO GALATIANS 5:16-26

Purpose
To apply the GPS-Method to Galatians 5:16-26

The Bible GPS-Method takes us through the processes of UNDERSTANDING, APPLICATION AND COMMUNICATION

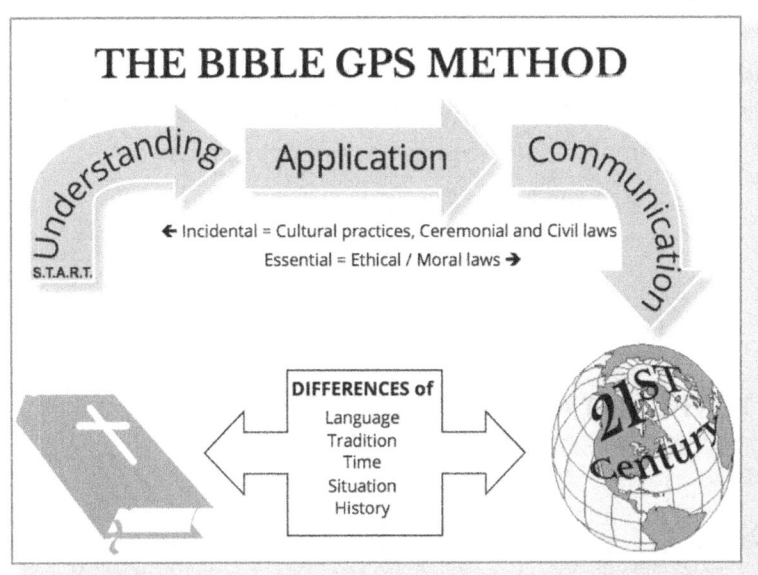

A. THE PROCESS OF UNDERSTANDING (S.T.A.R.T.)

We use the acronym "START" to determine how the original receivers of Galatians understood the message.

1. SITUATION

_____

_____

2. TYPE OF LITERATURE _____

3. ANALYSIS OF THE PASSAGE

      3.1 Write out the passage into smaller units (see page 83)

      3.2 Mark the main themes (zoom in)

      3.3 Explain difficult words and phrases (if necessary)

      3.4 Summarize the main sections in your own words (zoom out)

      3.5 Conclude and summarize the message to the original receiver

      _____

      _____

4. RELATIONSHIP TO THE REST OF THE BIBLE

  Romans 8:5 & 2 Corinthians 5:17

      YES _____ NO _____

5. TEST OF YOUR FINDINGS

Does the finding of others (e.g. commentaries, study Bibles) confirm the message to the original receiver?

      YES _____ NO _____

Galatians 5: 16-26

[16] So I say, live by the Spirit,
and you will not gratify the desires of the sinful nature.
[17] For the sinful nature desires
what is contrary to the Spirit,
and the Spirit what is contrary to the sinful nature.
They are in conflict with each other,
so that you do not do what you want.
[18] But if you are led by the Spirit,
you are not under law.
[19] The acts of the sinful nature are obvious:
sexual immorality, impurity and debauchery;
[20] idolatry and witchcraft;
hatred, discord, jealousy, fits of rage,
selfish ambition, dissensions, factions [21] and envy;
drunkenness, orgies, and the like.
I warn you, as I did before,
that those who live like this
will not inherit the kingdom of God.
[22] But the fruit of the Spirit is love, joy, peace, patience,
kindness, goodness, faithfulness,
[23] gentleness and self-control.
Against such things there is no law.
[24] Those who belong to Christ Jesus
have crucified the sinful nature
with its passions and desires.
[25] Since we live by the Spirit,
let us keep in step with the Spirit.
[26] Let us not become conceited,
provoking and envying each other. (NIV)

B. THE PROCESS OF APPLICATION

In this process, we determine whether or not the message to the original receiver is still applicable (essential or incidental) to our present situation.

You must distinguish the difference between an INCIDENTAL and an ESSENTIAL message.

We saw in Lesson 4 that only the Moral (Ethical) Laws are essential and, therefore, applicable to us.

Civil Laws	Ceremonial Laws	Cultural Practices	Moral Law

PURPOSE

Regulating the nation of Israel	Animal sacrifices to make atonement for sin. Point to Christ, the true Lamb	Comprise the ways people do certain things	Universal guidelines telling us how to live

EXAMPLE

Building regulations (Deut 22:8)	The Passover (Lev 16)	To greet with a kiss. (1 Peter 5:14)	The Ten Commandments (Ex 20)

Is the message to the original receivers applicable to us in the 21st century?

YES _____ NO _____

C. THE PROCESSES OF COMMUNICATION

In this process we communicate the message to a specific target group.

Questions for Group Discussion

- Did the lesson help you to master the processes of Understanding, Application and Communication?

  A friend contacts you and shares the following:

  > *"You know, I'd like to share something with you which I have never shared with anyone before. I have decided to share it with you because I trust you.   You see, there is within me a raging civil war. It drives me crazy!*

  > *I want to live a good life, but before I could help myself, I visited some web pages, which I know are not good. I also easily lose my temper, especially when watching how my favorite team loses. There are many other things I am struggling with. I do not know what to do and I'm afraid God will punish me."*

- Do you think the person's struggle is unique or is it something we all struggle with (Romans 7:19)?

- What do you think of his reference to his struggle as a "civil war?"

- How will you answer your friend according to Galatians 5:16-26?

- "The greatest conflicts are not between two people but between one person and himself?" (Garth Brooks, American country singer) Discuss the quote.

- Share blessings and prayer requests and pray for one another.

LESSON 7
THE GPS-METHOD APPLIED TO EPHESIANS 5:8-20

Purpose
To apply the GPS-Method to Ephesians 5:8-20

The Bible GPS-Method takes us through the processes of UNDERSTANDING, APPLICATION AND COMMUNICATION

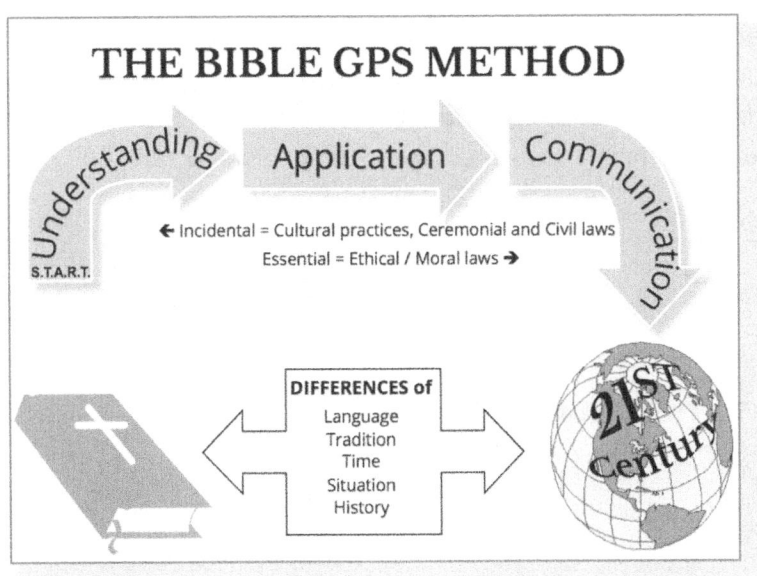

A . THE PROCESS OF UNDERSTANDING (S.T.A.R.T.)

We use the acronym "START" to determine how the original receivers of Galatians understood the message.

1. SITUATION

_____

_____

2. TYPE OF LITERATURE _____

3. ANALYSIS OF THE PASSAGE

      3.1 Write out the passage into smaller units (see page 83)

      3.2 Mark the main themes (zoom in)

      3.3 Explain difficult words and phrases (if necessary)

      3.4 Summarize the main sections in your own words (zoom out)

      3.5 Conclude and summarize the message to the original receiver

      _____

      _____

4. RELATIONSHIP TO THE REST OF THE BIBLE

   Romans 8:5 & 2 Corinthians 5:17

      YES _____ NO _____

5. TEST OF YOUR FINDINGS

Does the finding of others (e.g. commentaries, study Bibles) confirm the message to the original receiver?

      YES _____ NO _____

Ephesians 5: 8-20

[8] At one time you were in the dark.

But now you are in the light

because of what the Lord has done.

Live like children of the light.

[9] The light produces what is completely good,

right and true.

[10] Find out what pleases the Lord.

[11] Have nothing to do with the acts of darkness.

They don't produce anything good.

Show what they are really like.

[12] It is shameful even to talk about what people who don't obey do in secret.

[13] But everything the light shines on can be seen.

[14] Light makes everything clear.

That is why it is said,

"Wake up, sleeper. Rise from the dead. Then Christ will shine on you."

[15] So be very careful how you live.

Do not live like people who aren't wise.

Live like people who are wise.

[16] Make the most of every opportunity.

The days are evil.

[17] So don't be foolish.

Instead, understand what the Lord wants.

[18] Don't fill yourself up with wine.

Getting drunk will lead to wild living.

Instead, be filled with the Holy Spirit.

[19] Speak to each other with psalms, hymns and spiritual songs.

Sing and make music in your heart to the Lord.

[20] Always give thanks to God the Father for everything.

Give thanks to him in the name of our Lord Jesus Christ.

[26] Let us not become conceited,

provoking and envying each other. (NIV)

B. THE PROCESS OF APPLICATION

In this process, we determine whether or not the message to the original receiver is still applicable (essential or incidental) to our present situation.

You must distinguish the difference between an INCIDENTAL and an ESSENTIAL message.

We saw in Lesson 4 that only the Moral (Ethical) Laws are essential and, therefore, applicable to us.

Civil Laws	Ceremonial Laws	Cultural Practices	Moral Law

PURPOSE

Regulating the nation of Israel	Animal sacrifices to make atonement for sin. Point to Christ, the true Lamb	Comprise the ways people do certain things	Universal guidelines telling us how to live

EXAMPLE

Building regulations (Deut 22:8)	The Passover (Lev 16)	To greet with a kiss. (1 Peter 5:14)	The Ten Commandments (Ex 20)

Is the message to the original receivers applicable to us in the 21st century?

YES _____ NO _____

C. THE PROCESSES OF COMMUNICATION

In this process we communicate the message to a specific target group.

Questions for Group Discussion

- Did the lesson help you to master the processes of Understanding, Application and Communication?

    Scenario:
    You meet a great person while camping. One night at campfire the conversation lead to a serious discussion. In the light of this passage (and other passages), how would you have answered the following questions that were raised by your friend during the course of the discussion?

    Questions of friend:

- Why is the world in such a mess?

- What is the answer to this mess?

- My child is hanging out with the wrong crowd. My wife and I just don't know what to do anymore. He /she has so much potential and causes us so much pain by the foolish things he/she does. We lack some wisdom. What do you think we need to do.

- Share blessings and prayer requests and pray for one another.

About the Author

KOBUS GENIS was born in Bellville, South Africa. He obtained a Bachelor's Degree in Theology (BTh) from the University of Stellenbosch, South Africa, and served as a minister in South Africa from 1992-2003.

Since 2003 he and his family have been living in sunny Alberta, Canada, where he is a minister at Westminster Presbyterian Church, Calgary. Kobus' passion is to teach people how to UNDERSTAND, APPLY and COMMUNICATE the essentials of the Bible in the 21st century.

He is the author of two Devotionals: *From a Garden to a City* and *@Godstweet* as well as a discipleship book: *The Bible GPS.*

www.thebiblegps.com
https://www.facebook.com/BibleGPS

BIBLE
GPS

37487973R00057

Made in the USA
Middletown, DE
28 February 2019